CW01095277

First published in Great Britain in 1998 by
POETRY NOW
1-2 Wainman Road, Woodston,
Peterborough, PE2 7BU
Telephone (01733) 230746
Fax (01733) 230751

HB ISBN 0 75430 537 6
SB ISBN 0 75430 538 4

FOREWORD

Although we are a nation of poetry writers we are accused of not reading poetry and not buying poetry books: after many years of listening to the incessant gripes of poetry publishers, I can only assume that the books they publish, in general, are books that most people do not want to read.

Poetry should not be obscure, introverted, and as cryptic as a crossword puzzle: it is the poet's duty to reach out and embrace the world.

The world owes the poet nothing and we should not be expected to dig and delve into a rambling discourse searching for some inner meaning.

The reason we write poetry (and almost all of us do) is because we want to communicate: an ideal; an idea; or a specific feeling. Poetry is as essential in communication, as a letter; a radio; a telephone, and the main criteria for selecting the poems in this anthology is very simple: they communicate.

Enchanted Verse is a collection that focuses on a variety of topics, from the joy of a summer holiday, to a detailed account on the world's conflicting opinions.

Enchanted Verse is so diverse that everyone will find something to interest them and seize their imagination, whether they are a dedicated poetry lover or a first time reader. The soul, passion and inspiration of new and established poets have come together to create an anthology that captures the essence of life in a few short pages.

CONTENTS

FAREWELL

I cannot reach you with my hand,
Yet in my heart, I know you understand
For I have died a thousand times - yet live,
To feel your gentle touch - what would I give?
The agony of life, lives on
My love for you,
So very true and strong.
Now as I stand alone, and dream anew
I know that I shall die -
Still loving you!

T G Bloodworth

HOW TO MANAGE A YOUNG BRIDE - 1765

My mother in her wisdom said
'Come home dear son, 'tis time to wed
Leave those loose women of the town
'Tis time that you were settling down.
Seventeen is fine, a pure young dove
Is at the age to dream of love;
The innocent bride you can refine
And discipline to your design.
For horse and carriage, bed and board,
A wife's indebted to her lord.
Obedience is a husband's right
Whether by day or bedded at night.

Now if by chance your winsome filly
Should disobey and act quite silly
Do not let her rear and prance
And lead you in a devil's dance
The law permits you to chastise
A wilful wife who is unwise;
Subjected to the shock of pain
She'll soon respond to bit and reign
A girl and a filly all much akin,
Both wild and nervous 'neath the skin
But mount her now and sit astride
And ride your timid and willing bride!'

My mother's caution proved too right,
My marriage started with a blight
I took the sweet child to the city -
Which soon turned out to be a pity
She entreated me to buy her a gown
And then went out to search the town
For silks and satins, lace and frills
Landing me a clutch of bills.

Wantonly she'd spent my money
And spread her bread with jam and honey.
She let me cup her sweet white breast,
But gave no access to the rest!
Too long she'd made her lover wait
Less he exploit her virgin state.
She had no right to lock her door,
What did she think I had married her for?

Her excuses now were unavailing,
I'd grown tired of sweet persuading
So whipped her soundly till she cried,
My poor and foolish little bride!
Later humbled, contrite and sore
She wished she known what lay in store
Shyly she perched upon my knee
And rendered up her cherished key.
Lightly shriven with a kiss
She's borne aloft for nuptial bliss.
It was no crime to beat my wife,
It opened up a fruitful life
We love and sport now at our leisure
While she accommodates my pleasure.
She's happy as a lark all day
And welcomes all our amorous play.
She even, in quite scant attire,
Chases me to our secret bower.
She's learned her duties upstairs and down
She wears a bonnet, I the crown!

Anon

FRAGILE TEARS

Soft, fragile are the flowing tears of all those destined to sadly weep,
For so many innocents, who turn cold beneath the soil in restless sleep.
A grave week has laboured since last Saturday's loss, at ten past three,
From Market Street, in a neat country town thought by all to be so free.
Not to be forgotten are the living mementoes, in hospital with
torn limbs,
Scared faces and scared minds, adapting to empty spaces for their shins.
Tales of agony stab, for so many without a care, forfeited their
tomorrow.
Their loved ones left to drink the pain of such a deeply lamented
sorrow.
Lost lives, lost futures, lost hopes, lost jewels from life's
precious crown,
So many needlessly sacrificed to impair forever, Omagh, a
broken town.
Deep words of anger fester in the hearts of men, lying
now unexpressed.
Pure thoughts dwell solely on those who weep, still suffer, seek to rest.
All Ireland pauses this very day to pay its homage to the untimely dead.
Tears melt in the streams of mourners; heavy feet drag anchors of lead.
Unified in grief a country kneels to pray for many sins of
deep omission.
The darkest sin is that those so hurt, did not confer a willing permission.
Their sacrifices were offered by ungodly hands to sanction a
cruel cause.
It's time for all to examine their minds and manacle evil's deadly claws.

T Burke

QUESTION

If this was an atheistic world
And man shared no belief
Would this ensure a unity
And terrorism cease.

In whose name would we slaughter
Children, cherished and loved
Religion holds no impunity
From God's judgement up above.

Lay down your swords of hated steel
Let no life be defamed
Then maybe we can dwell with peace
On this God's earth again.

No coffin draped with garlands
Can further hatreds cause
But stain the cross where Jesus died
The son of Christ, our Lord.

G J Hutchings

MEMORIES

The wind blows softly through the trees,
as I turn to focus my eyes on the sea.
The peace that is around me cannot be denied,
but still to myself I lie.

I tell myself that he no longer exists,
and won't enter my heart again.
But when the wind blows I hear his name,
and see his shadow on the sand.

As the sun sets, I lie again,
denying that I am in pain.
The only truth that I can face is that I've lost him.

But during this time he's with me still,
alive, deep in my heart.
I try to push him away,
but do not succeed.

The first stars appear, in their twinkling glory,
which makes me think of his eyes.
The eyes that held so much passion,
and in his last moments, fear.

I walk down onto the seaweed covered rock,
to bow my head down and weep.
As the tears roll down, I feel a release,
now he has gone from my heart.
But will always be in my memories.

Antoinette Barnes

THE DIANA WALTZ

(To a beautiful dancing girl)
Take the floor for the Diana Waltz:
The beautiful Diana Waltz.
Glide and sway gracefully
As a sweet memory
Strums joy on the strings of your heart.

Let toes twinkle like stars up above:
To musical bars that we love.
Making each one, two three
Light as feathers to be
The breathtaking steps of the scene.

And as danced is the night far away
To orchestra's merry soiree:
May this waltz of delight
Bid you fondly goodnight:
The melody filling sweet dreams.

So honour your partner, and dance with me
The beautiful Diana Waltz, the sweet waltz:
The beautiful Diana Waltz.
The whirliest, twirliest, dear boy and girliest,
Beautiful Diana Waltz, sweet waltz,
The beautiful Diana Waltz.

Violet M Corlett

UNTITLED

I've had it torn out
Once or twice
I am devout
To God and Christ
My heart my heart
How you cry
And mourn
Since that day
When I was born

Philip Allen

NORTHERN IRELAND

It is time to stop
Time to try
A new way forward
And none to die
It is time to wave
Goodbye to fame
Of wicked people
You cannot name
Who fight and fight
Without real reason
Who kill the innocent
Each passing season
For Patrick won't knock
At the door anymore
Mary and Peter cannot
Call again
Great 'Father' Lewis lies
Dead in his bed
Killed by devil followers -
Sick thoughts
In their head.

Peter Mitchell

War - A Case Of Conflict

I stood with arms erect at war
On a battleship's signal platform chore
A message to pass to outer screen
Of destroyer, cruising in that scene

With fear that only battles show
With gunfire smoke, shells' afterglow
Splattered bodies all about
As angered men bawl and shout

A whizzing by my ears just then
Mere eight inch shells, yer ken!
For every shell, driving past
Missing me - hitting mast!

As smoke clears - in my view
Enemy ship and sweating crew
Battle on with yell and shout
This is wartime's general bout.

Message passed Sir, captain to respect
Carry on signalmen, kept erect
Onto anti-aircraft gun
Attempt to shoot down every Hun!
War benefits no man alive or dead
Wasted years on the enemy fled
All we but later looking back
Are wasted efforts in our track.

The enemies we so gallantly fought,
All our efforts - we often thought
For King and country - I declare
Was wasted effort - and I dare.
Tell grandchildren
Be aware!

Yet at those who lead us now
As to our war enemies they bow
Remember you - our mates who died
To keep away the enemy and tide!
We will remember them - we cried!
Britain's nation our pride!

Geoffrey Wilyman

TROPICAL ISLAND

We journeyed two hours to the hotel by taxi
On the unmade roads, nearly having apoplexy
As surrounding area appeared impoverished,
Countryside was flat and the earth undernourished.

Flown thousands of miles to destination,
In preparation suffered vaccination,
It seemed we must expect disappointment,
Felt reluctant to keep hotel appointment.

Turned into a serpentine drive the entrance, spherule,
Doors opened into carpeted vast vestibule,
Huge stairway to opulent reception, like film set,
Opposite thoughts than those on rough drive at outset.

Staff, calf-skirted men, women, majestic,
Amazon, handsome, muscular, athletic,
Relaxing, flashing smiles, utterly content,
Happiest of people that was evident.

Views, coconut palm trees, azure sea and golden sand,
Inviting hammocks slung, sunloungers unmanned,
On beach sparkling waves gently overlapped,
Water crystal clear as from mountain, snow-capped.

A bar erected in the swimming pool
Also sold ice-creams to keep pampered guests cool,
Tropical flower gardens, magical,
Setting so perfect nighly theatrical.

Peaceful, tranquil except for swish and hack in the trees,
To axe nuts a man shinned the trunk, rustled crown leaves,
Returns, lops the tops, thrusts in straws, offers juice milk,
Quenches thirst, tastes sweet and luscious, iced cool as silk.

Fiji, dream island in the Pacific,
Remembered yearningly it is idyllic.

Hilary Jill Robson

KILCHOMEN

Kilchomen
the summer Islay holiday eerie
of the Lords' of the isles; now long since gone.
Yet the high standing Kilchomen Cross still
projects earth to heaven, stone hallowing
the birthplace of Christianity on
these shores. Church dilapidated - worship
no longer safe within its old stone walls.
Environment beautiful, wild, nature
ruling naturally in its deep praise.
God supreme.

Robert D Shooter

THE GIFT

Two young ladies, well aware,
Attracted every gaze.
Different in their ages, yet,
Alike in many ways.
One was elegant in pink,
The other all in white
And holding court that day they made
A truly joyful sight.

I'd loved them both for many years
And knew that they loved me,
But I could not keep both of them,
One wanted to be free.
Now, my wife smiled at the groom
On this their special day.
My daughter put her hand in mine
And I gave her away . . .

Frank Jensen

INSPIRATION

The poet, sat by the fireside,
Waiting for inspiration,
Then to his brain he applied,
A most painful operation.

Outside, the moon shone brightly,
Stars twinkled, as if to say -
The shadows dance so spritely,
As it's the ending of this day!

Longing for pen to contact paper,
Waiting for inspiration to come,
The poet sat still; waiting - waiting . . .
But no inspiration would come!

Hannah Gale (10)

The Mouse That Loved To Travel

The little mouse stood on the dock
His suitcase in his hand
He looked at his watch, then at the sky
And concluded life was grand.

'Should I go by plane or boat
I like the idea of being afloat
To fly would be a wonderful thing
Like riding high upon a swing'

A boat sailed by he got on board
And settled in the cold dark hold
Unwrapping his sandwiches he started to munch
On cheese and pickles he'd packed for lunch

He poured himself a cup of tea
And sat musing in happy reverie
'I'll go on deck and see the sights
Before I nestle down for the night'

A slight rustle was heard behind the sacks
Sending shivers of fear right down his back
Speaking nervously he tried to be bold

He raised his umbrella high in defence
Thinking surely this makes no sense
A cat would pounce, not wait so long
When from the corner, he heard a song

A pretty song with a quite sad air
Was being sung by a mouse so fair
'My name is Lucy, Sir,' she spoke in a hurry
'I'm sorry to give you need to worry'

'Why that's alright' he said with a grin
'Shall we sit awhile then we can begin
If you like I'll escort you to see the sights
But we must be quick, before darkness of night'

They journeyed to Egypt on the boat
Falling in love while they were afloat
They married at once and looked to the sky
On the way back, he said 'We'll fly.'

Now their children sit and listen
With noses twitching and eyes that glisten
To tales of countries far away
And dream of going there some day.

Ann Bell

REMEMBRANCE

Within four walls, where silence is kept,
I find your shadow lies where you once slept,
And each night I know if I look around,
Sweet thoughts and memories are to be found,
To each little oddment I find a thought,
And to the happiness that they have brought
But with all that there still remains,
Little left that is the same
When I close the door upon it all,
I hear a voice within there call,
'Come back and with shadow lie
Love like ours will never die'

One instance of God's work in my life stands out in my memory.
Due to mounting pressures in my life, my energies were slowly
ebbing away, and love for God was far from my mind, applied to
my stormy situation. The Lord sent me strength from above,
kept me from sinking beneath waves of human weakness.
Oh how I loved him then, not only because he had given me
strength, but because God was my strength. I think back to the Lord's
special work in my life, I call on him for today's needs,
I will love you O Lord, my God.
Oh help me Lord, to take by grace divine, yet more and more of
that great love of thine, that day by day my heart may give to thee,
a deeper love, and flow more constantly.

Olive Powell

POOR OLD TED

I'm only a manky old teddy bear
And not only that, I've only one ear
I've had lots of hugs,
And plenty of kisses
From little girls and boys
To misters and misses.
I've been thrown in the cupboard,
Kicked out of bed.
I'm only a harmless little ted
I've had my head stood on
I've had my nose hit
I can't fight back
Not one little bit
My coat is all torn
My fur is all worn
My stuffing is all hanging out
But a Ted is a Ted
And I won't complain
Because that's what loving's about.

Jeffrey Shedlow

You Will Never Know

Sitting here at midnight
I've said my last goodbyes
'I love you Grandad' I whisper
Tears in my eyes

You didn't even know me
But that is the way cancer works
To say goodbye for the last time
You'll never know how that hurts

You were like a father
And a dearest friend
You'll never know how much it hurts
To know it's going to end

So goodbye dearest Grandad
You'll always be in my heart
Even though I know very soon
We will be apart.

Lorraine Bridgwater

MY SUMMER TREAT!

I've been to Spain and Italy!
America was swell!
Both New Zealand and New Guinea,
I knew them kind of well!
I've been to Russia and to France!
South Africa was grand!
This year I thought I'd take a chance
And see the Holy Land!
Because I've worked for months on end
And Spring is almost done,
I think of all the days I'll spend
On holiday! What fun!
Whatever truths God will impart
I'll honour them for sure!
God's Spirit lives within my heart -
The Saviour to adore!
Jerusalem, I'm coming soon!
(Thank God the money's paid!)
Jerusalem, two weeks in June!
For you I've prayed and prayed!
I'll visit all your holy sites
Along my Christian tour . . .
Ask God to bless the Israelites . . .
Reflect upon God's Law . . .
Remember Jesus, King of Kings . . .
The Cross of Christ He braved . . .
And then, of course, above all things,
Praise God, through Him, I'm saved!

Denis Martindale

Day-Trippers

The gentle tide
Dozes in the heat,
Lulling her crooning
Waves to sleep
About the sandy bay.

If only they would
Stay away,
I'd languish here
All day, instead of
Turning and running away.

Adrian Covill

BACK IN 1982

Some years ago we decided to have a break
A week away just us two to take
So while one was having a nap
I stuck a pin in the map
Nothing to shout about for glee
It landed on the south coast at Southsea
Not one of the sunnier climes that come to mind
But really we should not be so unkind
Fortunately it was a very pleasant week
Fine weather, many places to seek
Portsmouth the Victory in all its glory
History abound could give many a story
Hayling Island a long walk of a trek
Here there was no such wreck
Just two worn out hot bodies
Waiting to be transported on trolleys
Getting the bus back to the hotel for a shower
Although transport took nearly an hour
Days all sorted out for us to be
On the hovercraft over to Ryde on the sea
Isle of Wight beckons for a further trek
Carisbrooke Castle don't break your neck
There was no waste on our holiday to teach
As the next day we spent on the beach
Major attraction of the last day
Navy returning from the Falklands to stay
HMS Invincible and Bristol, helicopters up high
Streams of red, white and blue smoke in the sky
Something to savour just us two
When this all happened back in 1982.

Anthony Higgins

THE IDLE PEACOCK

We had journeyed far in spray of rain
to view demesne of Scone;
the tale was told of stolen stone -
where then it lay.
In truth, to me, such bore no shock -
sackers oft' claim 'symbols' as their own!

Yet castle showed none of its past pain,
for in extensive grounds
grew trees which recognised no bounds
which on *this* May
introduced to me a peacock
from deep shadows which the eyes did confound.

Then, as the sun yawned . . . and stretched again
bright mighty healing arms,
deciding that we meant no harm -
and seemed not fey -
emerged this wary gem to mock
the drab silent starers with his charms.

From the leaf-dappled shade he did deign
to near our picnic bench
as, mesmerised, the seat I clenched -
blessing the day
this wonder breathed, cursing the clock
which chimed time to leave, when with sad wrench
I bade my soft farewells
to quit the mystical gardens
wherein dwelled the idle peacock

Perry McDaid

MY SUMMER HIDEAWAY

There is a very special place
I like to call my own.
A place to sit and contemplate
Where I can be alone!
It's peaceful and yet full of life,
So busy, and yet calm,
Somewhere to rest and dream awhile
Away from any harm!
There's my beautiful cat asleep on his back,
As I watch him, I can't help but smile
As the heat of the sun warms up his tum
And he stretches himself like a mile!
There's butterflies and bumble bees
There's lots of trees and plants,
A rockery, a strawberry bush,
And of course just one or two ants!
The air is filled with the sweet perfume
Of glorious summer flowers
For this is my own garden
Where I while away the hours!

Charmaine S Dawson

LOCHGOILHEAD COLOURS

The mist lifts up,
revealing a magical place.
The sun shines down,
reflecting off the waterfalls,
blinding me with the colours of the rainbow,
like a ray of pure magic.

The water from the mountain high
charges down the hillside.
Plants grow from the wet surroundings,
thickly from the soil,
all the rocks covered in
a thick carpet of velvet moss.
The light from this amazing wonder,
making everything green.

The loch looks green,
the rocks are green,
the rivers are fountains of green gold.
And as I walk I can't see why
I should go back to the grey of the city.

A Konczak (15)

WHATEVER THE WEATHER

Sitting on the beach with scarf around my neck,
The north wind is blowing here, but oh well what the heck!
This is where, in summertime, my family likes to be,
We come here for the donkey rides, the ice cream and the sea.

When it's raining hard, we still find lots to do:
Play in the amusements to pass an hour or two.
My dad likes ten-pin bowling, it is his favourite game.
He's getting really good at it, a star of the fast lane!

On a sunny day, there's Kinderland for fun.
My sister likes the swings and slides - lots for playing on.
In Atlantis Waterpark, a place for cooling down,
There is a Pirate's Cove and slide - the biggest in the town.

I love the seafood here, it makes a tasty dish:
Lobster, mussels, prawns and crabs, all different kinds of fish.
A visit to the harbour bar with lots of treats in store:
Ice cream sundaes, melbas, jellies and a whole lot more!

My mum goes to the shops, if she's some time in hand
Once we've been to a show or the Spa to hear the band.
There are many things to do and just no time to rest . . .
There is no doubt, my mind's made up, that Scarborough is the best!

Laura Eastwood (12)

DOWN THE CHALET

On a lazy summer's day
There's no better place to be
Than in my grandad's chalet
At Leysdown on sea.

There's always lots to do there
Whether indoors or outside.
On my own or with my sisters,
There's even bikes to ride.

We've been playing all the morning
In the pleasant summer heat
But now we're getting hungry
What shall we have to eat?

The Cosy Cafe serves wonderful meals
Like lasagne, chips and peas
But I look forward to deserts most,
Chocolate fudge cake, please!

We spend the afternoon at the beach
And paddling in the sea.
Playing on the fruit machines
Wow! I've won 2p.

Then later in the evening
When the sun begins to fade
We head towards the local pub,
For crisps and lemonade.

Louisa Burkin (13)

YESTERDAY

As dawn crept in on silent feet
with gentle spots of rain
Dad took our cases down the street
to catch the early train.
The train to steam away, both far and fast
our Dorset holiday begun at last.

It was as if the train stood still,
the world was rushing by.
I still recall the vibrant thrill
that passed before my eye.
The rhythm changed and I became aware
the train was slowing . . . we were almost there.

There was no sun on that first day,
waves splashed on dull wet sand.
The grey horizon far away,
no chance of getting tanned.
But neither wind nor rain could bother me
as long as I could be there, by the sea.

And then, cloud curtain rearranged,
the sun came streaming through.
Before my eyes, the whole scene changed,
gold sand, a sea of blue.
You asked me where I'd love to be the most.
I'll tell you . . . Swanage, on the Dorset coast.

Roger Brougham

ISLE OF MAN

Talk to me so I cannot think
Of watching filmy water shrink
Across the nutmeg sand of Peel
And, surely, they only must be real -
The hay field steep above the sea,
The fuschia and the daisy tree?

And warm grass on the Chasms' path;
And many a leaving's aftermath;
And patchwork land, and the children's voices
Of birds on the cliffs; and children's choices;
And the long lane to the Lonan Church?
And, where, in Lancashire, shall I search?

Christine Roberts

MY FAVOURITE PLACE

My favourite place in the summer is to lie beside the pool,
Enjoying the peace on a tropical island before we go back to school.
I love to be on holiday soaking up the sun,
Reading a book by the pool and having lots of fun.
The reason this is my favourite place,
Is because it puts a smile on my face.
It is where I like to rest,
And have a fun time which is simply the best!

Kim Adams (12)

MY SUNSHINE POEM

On every summer holiday,
I went to sunny Spain.
Because the food and weather over here,
Just wasn't the same.
I loved the entertainment,
The sun, sand and sea,
Spain was a lovely country,
A beautiful place to be.
You could go on excursions,
And eat chicken and chips.
Or pizza or lasagne,
I really enjoyed my trips!
The thing I liked most
About it all,
Was to play in the sea,
With my small bat and ball.
I loved my sunny summers,
When I went to Spain,
Because when I came back
It usually started to rain!
But I thoroughly enjoyed,
My summers over there.
This summer I'm going somewhere else
In Portugal somewhere!
So here's to sunny Spain,
The place I love the best
I went there every summer
Spain is better than the rest!

Claire Hall (13)

THE SOCIETY FOR NUDE POETRY READING?

This report from the nude room.
Down London they have started nude poetry reading clubs
well you know what they're like down south.
London. Leg-Over—Now-Dear-Or-Never,
well that's what London stands for up north.
You stand there in the nude and read your poetry out to all the audience
the audience are sat there in the nude too letting it all hang out.
Just think you are stood there reading poetry out to all
then you get a funny feeling and they all see you've got a pan handle on
they call it body language it helps express your poetry.
Then a lady in the audience eating a 99 ice cream
she drops the 99 ice cream and a flake on a brown man's lap.
What a shock cold ice cream all down his legs -
she tries to clean up the mess. That's not the 99's flake Miss
you've got hold of, it's the brown man's stick of rock.
You are stood up there reading your poetry out you look around the
audience. All the men are sat there legs open and all the women
with their legs shut. Well ladies you will see all the men who need
Viagra pills and all the men who don't, and when the poetry reading's
over and they all stand up to give you a clap,
the ladies who have been holding their wind in will play you a tune too
100 bums vibrating 100 smells around the room.
Nude poets with pegs on their noses running from the room
and then the poetry reading's over and off you all go home
to sit around the fire and discuss the nude poetry reading club.

Donald Jay

THE LITTLE TOY CLOWN

The little clown sat on the toy box
feeling really down.
'I wish they'd sew my buttons on,'
he said with a frown.
'They won't bother with you'
said a doll nearby.
'you're much too tatty.'
That made him cry.
'They're throwing all the old toys out
you'll be the next to go.'
That really worried him,
he felt full of woe.
Then Jill came along,
she sat him in a chair,
took off his hat
and combed his hair.
She carried him downstairs
and handed him to Mum.
'Could you repair him?
He looks so glum.'
So out came the sewing machine,
Mum worked all night,
replacing his buttons,
what a splendid sight!
She made him a brand new set of clothes,
and stitched up his ears,
when the other toys saw him,
they greeted him with cheers.
There was no more teasing,
he wouldn't be thrown away,
yes - he knew
they would let him stay.

Wendy Watkin

THE TRIAL OF A MAN CHARGED WITH MEMBERSHIP OF A PROSCRIBED ORGANISATION

Does he float upon the water
When his thumbs to toes are tied?
Does he scream aloud when pricked with pins
Or take it in his stride?
Are there shamrock marks upon his skin?
For these, we know attract
Familiars and this proves
All allegations to be fact
He will not name, for his salvation
Other members of the team?
Indisputable the evidence
Against him, it would seem!
Taken with the trusted word
Of a chief constable, I'm sure
That this man must be a terrorist
For so says British law.

Kim Montia

OUR MOTHER

These soft green fingers of grass,
that hold and cradle me,
as I lay here,
a child in mother's arms,
gazing up at her beautiful freckled face,
the open, moonlit, starry night,
I lay here with peace,
as she caresses my face tenderly,
with her soft brushing breath,
and I am her captive,
as the Midas touch of sunlight,
turning black and grey into yellow and gold,
sweeps away the shadows of night,
in the opening of her one tranquil eye,
whilst beneath this sea of emotion,
my diluvial personality cries,
'I don't love you enough,
our beautiful yet unforgiving mother.'

John Marshall

OUR DESTINY

An ill wind blows
Seeds of peace are scattered
In this wind of change
All dreams and hope lie shattered.

Reality unfolds with violence and crime
Talks are considered a waste of good time.
Children throw bombs, never thinking *why*
Hatred runs deep, 'Why us?' they cry.

But what is achieved? Heartache, pain
Lives that can never be normal again
Families divided, as smoke fills the sky
People with guns, say 'An eye for an eye.'

Common sense must prevail, sow the seeds once again
Let good conquer evil, as sun follows rain
Talks are no good, unless all sides agree
That weapons aren't needed, to set us all free.

Someday all this must be a thing of the past
Sort out the problems, then friendships shall last
Let's help one another in peace, harmony
Life is too short, it's our destiny . . .

GIG

SUNSHINE SURF AND SAND (TENERIFE)

I gaze at ripples, glinting, watch the sun
Send dancing rays through chinks of swaying palms
As blissfully I stretch a pallid limb
How wonderful life feels without such qualms

As clothing; shorts and T-shirt will suffice
No rain attire - no extra added weight
To lumber 'round except perhaps a book
And towel, if not to dry, just used to drape

Across the sun bed deemed to mark your spot
Before the rites begin - some rise at dawn
And make the choosing of their special space
A ritualistic duty to perform

But that aside, just knowing every day
Will be the same, is bliss, deep clear blue pool
White surf exploding close along the shore
Some long exotic drink to keep you cool

What more is there to life than sun and sea
A soft warm breeze above to gently fan
Those bodies stretched beneath a cloudless sky
Their one and only aim - to catch a tan

But just as we adjust to climate, taste,
And atmospheric wafts of cultures new
It's over - all too soon the week is up
With suitcase packed, we sadly bid adieu

And travel home to where it's damp and grey
Thick murky cloud surrounds us as we land
A voice inside determining next year
We'll take a month of sunshine surf and sand!

Jo Lewis

MY SUMMER PLACE

In the summer I like to be,
In the shade behind our apple tree,
It's cool and dark and all for me,
That's behind my apple tree,
On the tree grows tasty fruits,
And it has very long roots,
My mum makes great apple crumble,
It fills you up when your stomach will rumble,
It's a magical place to be,
In behind our apple tree.

Tom Sampson (12)

WAS IT A DREAM?

Is it a dream
Am I really here?
Where the girls are so pretty
With long dark hair

You walk among flora
Hibiscus, bougainvillaea
Bamboo and palms and
Trees of poinsettia.

There are fruits in abundance
At stalls and on trees
Mango, banana
Jackfruit and papaya.

Palms wave over beaches
Of silver white sand
The azure blue sea
Where fish and coral abound.

By Banca we crossed a freshwater lake
To see a volcano at Taal
The winds increased and we got very wet
But good fun was had by us all

So now our vacation has come to an end
Events in our memory we store
I say to myself 'Was it in my dreams?'
Was I really there - in the Philippines?

Joyce M Carter

CHRISTMAS TIME

Christmas is that time of year
To be close to families that are so dear
The tree, the fire, tinsel and bows
Which bring such warmth to icy toes
The mistletoe kisses and sherry and beer
All add to that annual Christmas cheer
All the small children tucked up in bed
Dreaming of Santa, his reindeer and sled
The sparkle of Christmas will always be
The merriest time of the year for me.

Claire Bellamy

A SPECIAL PLACE

Soft golden sands of a quiet Norfolk beach
around the Wash where the sea is out of reach.
Miles of beaches with the tide so far out
but the wet sand is fun, without any doubt.
People carrying buckets, as there are cockles galore,
where to laze or paddle is the only chore.
My favourite of them all is Holkham Bay
with its secluded dunes where you can lay.

Acres of woodland surrounds this lovely place
a sanctuary for birds, flying with grace.
A nature reserve for everyone to enjoy at its very best
where animals can breed, safe and secure in their nests.
All around Norfolk are places like this,
places of natural beauty which no one should miss.

Carole Bloomfield

SUMMER FAVOURITES

My favourite place for a summer holiday
Is the land where the seagulls cry,
And red hot sunrays covering the bay
Descending from the sky.

Glistening waters full of fun and memories of by-gone years,
Immerse me in its clearness
My worries all disperse.

An evening meal down a cobbled street
The 'Cobble Stones' restaurant,
Or the 'Ventura', an Italian place
Accompanied by candlelight.

Afterwards we take a stroll and watch the smooth low waves
And then return to our cosy flat,
Where the clear night behaves.

Next day, a trip to St Michael's Mount
Our family favourite visit,
Up the hundreds of steps we count
To the Giant's Heart exhibit.

And the mythical well in which the Giant fell
Is also there to see,
Along with the exotic flowers and smells
My kind of luxury.

Cornwall has these pleasures to possess
And many, many more,
Just one more thing I'm certain of,
I'll be back again for sure!

Helen Withington (14)

SURPRISE VISIT

Down on the beach the helicopter flew
With the pilot and three members of the crew.
It was a sight I had not seen before -
A helicopter landing so close to the shore.

Children were amazed to see it landed there,
Ran over to see it stopped with a stare.
Out came three members of the crew,
Going to the job they had to do.

Time passed whilst they did the job,
Then into the sky it lifted and bobbed.
It was something you don't see every day,
Just wish you were here down this way.

Evelyn M Harding

CORNWALL

(In loving memory of Gran, Grandad, Aunty Kit and Uncle Phil.)

If I could choose anywhere
in the world to go on holiday,
it would be in Cornwall
this is where I would like to stay.

There are lots of different
places to visit in Cornwall, England.
Lots of nice, clean beaches,
and the beautiful light, golden sand.

It's nice to swim in the sea
or sunbathe on the beach.
Soaking up the warm sun,
until your skin turns peach.

If you like beautiful scenery,
and if you like the sun,
go to Cornwall for a break,
you will have lots of fun.

So when you book a holiday,
think how lovely Cornwall sounds.
Book a place here in England,
not abroad, it will save you pounds.

Janice Tucker

Moyra's Path

Think of a sunny path that went
Through tender Devon air,
Springy sprays of grass were bent
By those that ambled there,
That path was loved with tenderness
By hearts that leap at loveliness.
How do I know? Well, I was there,
And saw my Moyra love it,
With its innocent flowers, the salt sea air
And a gauze of gold upon it,
And the call it gave, pulling us on
To haunted cave and sea and sun.
For where did it go? Well, down to the sea,
With John already there,
And oh! the joy it gave us three,
For freshly everywhere,
Shining and wet, patterned and curled,
Were shells of every hue in the world.

Terence Belford

DREAM

Dream a dream,
yet stay awake,
lying upon,
the shore of a lake.

Stiff still water,
blazing sun,
soft silky sand,
the day has begun.

The beach is calm,
peaceful, relaxing;
the ice cold lake,
heavily tempting.

Fantasy, thoughts,
call it what you will,
lying on the beach,
there's dreams to fulfil.

Kristine Riley

OUR HOLIDAY

My family don't like holidays
They think they are a bore
I said we should go to Spain
Because there is sun and fun galore
But they don't like Spain
They think it's too hot
They said we could go to France for the World Cup
But they forgot
I said we could go to America
Because of Disneyland
But we couldn't
Because my brother couldn't take his one-man band
So I said we should go to Iceland
Because it's nice and cool
But they said
They would rather be in a pool
So last but not least I said we should go to a hotel
Because you can have a rest
But they said to stay in our house
Because it's the very best.

Grace Boyd (13)

VERY CLOSE TO MY HEART

Have you ever been to Llandudno?
With all its splendour.
When my children were growing up,
We had many happy holidays.
Photos in the dew to remind us of happy times.
Hotels stand tall on either side of the bay.
There's Great Orme and Little Orme,
You can't help seeing this.
There's Happy Valley, where people come to sing.
On a hill stands a church where people go to pray.
The graveyard looks over the sea,
With all its moods,
Calm gales and sunsets splendour.
Not far away is Conwy where people once would
Flock to see kings and queens crowned and beheaded.
Further down the cost is Caernarfon Castle
Where Prince Charles, he was narrated there.
I remember so clearly the Menai Bridge,
How beautiful it stands.
There's also Snowdon Mountain Railway,
Where everyone likes to have a ride on.
Not forgetting Mount Snowdon,
Most people like to climb.
Rhyl lies a few miles up the coast,
Where people flock to the funfair,
Spending all their money.
There's donkey rides, shops and cafes,
Punch and Judy makes the children laugh and shout.
There's lots to do and have some fun.
We mustn't forget the lifeguards patrolling the beach.
These are all deep memories,
Very close to my heart.

Jean Rickwood

SUMMERTIME

S un, sand and surf is what's lying ahead.
U p at dawn to keep a sunbed.
M ore parties and more fun until I collapse.
M ost definitely no more naps.
E very minute will be party time.
R age will turn into a crime.
T o enjoy my holiday is my main aim.
I 'll never have one the same.
M y hols next year will be even better still.
E ach year yet another thrill.

Louise Montgomery (14)

THE SUN

Show me a place where the sun beats down,
Amongst the silence in the town,
Where the sun's heat is at its highest peak,
All the hours, all the days and all week.

Marvellous colours, yellow, orange and red,
The soft smooth sand, a silky sunbed,
The rays glisten a sparkling light,
Do you hope to see the spellbinding sight?

This place you may want to see,
But it does not belong to you or me,
It has been put in a far away place,
Far too special for the human race.

Amy Fraser (11)

MY FAVOURITE PLACE

My favourite place,
In the sun is Lanzarote,
With all the fun,
Staying up late,
Singing and dancing,
Having loads of fun,
Sunbathing in the sun,
Jumping in the pool,
Snorkelling in the sea,
What is that I see?
It's a little fish,
Floating by,
One day left in the sunshine,
Sunbathe as much as you can!
As I watch the sun,
Fading in the distance,
I dread going back home,
The sad day comes,
For our return home,
I climb aboard the plane to
Take my seat,
I look from my window,
Lanzarote fades,
A few hours later we are home,
Where has Lanzarote gone?
My favourite Canary island.

Ashlee Brownell

SUMMER POEM

I like Italy,
Because it's hot.
The seasides are beautiful,
I like them a lot.

Bathing in the sunshine,
Swimming in the pool,
These things I like best of all.

Visiting the mountains,
Visiting the farms,
Seeing all the animals,
Having ice-creams in the bar.

Sitting in the Coliseum,
Staring at the domes,
Drinking from the fountains
Of Trevi in Rome.

Pizza and pasta,
Is my true delight,
Cannelloni and ravioli
Are also a wonderful sight.

It's so hot out there,
That you need your skimpy clothes,
So I warn you, to buy and get loads
Of shorts and T-shirts, bikinis and skirts,
Bring your suncream or you'll get burnt.

I hope you have a good time,
Use my advice,
'Cause I've been there many times . . .
So I know what it's like!

Natalie Faventi

SUNSHINE POEM

The sun is shining brightly in the sky
The fluffy candyfloss clouds sail on by
The earth is heated by the sun's soft rays
I love these happy summer days.

Birds float gently from tree to tree
Sitting in the rose bush is a bumble bee
Brightly coloured butterflies flutter silently through the air
On these warming summer days I don't have a care.

The flowers are in deep, deep bloom
The summer fruits will be ready to pick soon
Ice-creams are refreshing to eat
The tempting flavour is hard to beat.

The longer days and shorter nights
The beautiful sunsets red, purple and white
The summer is a beautiful season
The golden sunshine is the reason.

Gemma Dawson (14)

MY FAVOURITE PLACE ON A SUMMER'S DAY

O let me spend a summer's day,
    Around the town of Stornoway,
Let me relax and rest a while,
    There on that Hebridean isle.

I do not need to go abroad,
    For there I can be close to God,
Yet it too is across the sea,
    The place where I would like to be.

The castle on the hill up there
    Overlooks the harbour fair,
The rhododendrons in full bloom
    Have welcomed many an exile home.

Many changes now I see,
    In that place that's dear to me,
But on familiar sites I gaze,
    With memories of childhood days.

Unspoilt beaches close at hand,
    With blue-green sea and golden sand,
Not thronged with multitudes are they,
    E'en on the warmest summer's day.

At home with family and friends,
    I'd wish the day could never end;
My fav'rite place on a summer's day -
    My native town of Stornoway.

Donald J Mackay

A LITTLE OFFSHORE ISLAND ON THE SOUTH COAST OF ENGLAND

I like to be here
In the summer
When the sun beats
A path to my door -

I like to be here
To listen to the sea
Lapping upon
The shore -

I like to be here
As the seagulls screech,
Wending their way
To the beach -

I like to be here
When the crickets
Sing and dance
To their rhythmic beat -

I like to be here
Even when
There is no
Heat -

I like to be here
Because here is where
My heart is
And my heart lies deep -

Beverley Beck

BALI

Oh this is the place to be
So happy and so free
Sitting around the pool
In tropical Bali

Soaking up the sun
Surfing on the sea
Oh it is a great place to be
Tropical Bali

A warm summer breeze
Blowing through the palm trees
Sipping ice cold beer
In tropical Bali, here

So I want to thank you Lord
For all that you have given
For all the good times
That you have sent down from Heaven

For this lovely holiday
Of brightness and love
Thank you so very much my Lord
From your kingdom up above.

Jessica Wright

HEAVENLY BELLS

Floral boulevards . . . adorn, border the woodland glade,
Swaying, waving . . . sweet scented on the breeze.
Truly soporific . . . a beautiful bluebell wood . . .
Vital vista . . . green canopied, cobalt blue carpeted.

Nestling deep . . . in that sheltered, protected spot,
Safe, secure . . . from predators, man and nature.
Perfect panorama . . . it's 'picture-book' imagery,
Artist's paradise . . . a magic 'Monet-made' venue.

Cherished legacy . . . ours to protect and nurture,
Falling short . . . would render all . . . forever lost.
Drift amid . . . its dappled expansive blue sea,
Rest awhile . . . content amidst that intricate maze.

John Hirst

LIKE A RAINY SUMMER THAT WAS NEVER MEANT TO BE

(Dedicated to Nanna Mary and Dad Richie)

Like a rainy summer that was never meant to be,
I am frozen as a statue,
prisms of emptiness fill my eyes,
as no more salty tears can be shed.
A warm glowing ember burns deep inside,
and this is the memories that have embedded,
for you as a butterfly has flown into the distant horizon,
and every cloud in the distance can shine bright.
A star that shines so brightly,
a rainbow that blushes the sky,
dreams are for keeping,
and life is for sharing,
words mean nothing,
the sun keeps on shining.
Like a rainy summer that was never meant to be.

Donna Joanne Kinsey

MINI HOLIDAY

A gusting breeze blows sand, tormenting visitors who play,
delving deep in rock pools on a raw midsummer day,
investigating crevices,
wielding home-made rods,
scooping baby crabs in nets,
popping seaweed pods,
tug-of-warring limpet shells,
fingers turning blue,
noses glowing crimson,
cheeks flushed garish hue.

A chill wind shivers tiny hands, damp sand cakes, chafing toes,
though digging frenziedly with spades eliminates all woes,
and building sand pie castles tall,
adding windmill sails,
pouring water into moats,
hauling brimful pails,
puffing breath in water-wings,
braving ice cold dips,
licking dripping ice-cream cones,
scoffing fish and chips.

Salt tears combine with foaming surf as, hijacked by a wave,
fraught infant's beach ball drifts to sea to face a watery grave.
Threatening clouds bring leaden skies,
falling raindrops splash,
swooping gulls screech raucous cries,
heaving breakers crash.
But, towelled and dressed at breakneck speed,
crossing rain-soaked sand,
young day-trippers ignore the squall -
everything's been grand!

Maureen Atkin

SUMMER SNAPSHOTS

Cool stream
Sunbeam
Ice-cream
Daydream

Cold beer
Sky clear
Friends near
Much cheer

Sea air
Deckchair
Beachwear
Skin bare

Cut glass
Wine glass
Times pass
Peace, at last.

Polly Berrido

SUNDAY MORNING

A lazy sun just about to arise
On Sunday morning, yawning with stretch,
And rubbing his enormous eyes
After a jolly good sleep. Preacher began to preach
To his gathered flock; with church bells
Suddenly stopping to blare
Over quite village, except for the yells
Of happy children, laughing and shouting in spare.

Stanislaw Paul Debrowski-Oakland

JUST ME

I've a right to be
A part of the planet
Don't you see
I don't have to apologise
For what I am
A man or woman
Asexual
Don't have to bleed
'Cos I'm fat or thin
Don't have to grieve
If I don't fit in
A right to space
A right to air
A right to be
Just there.

Barbara Drake

JULY

July is a child with a butterfly net
'Don't coop it up in a jar, my pet'
July is the scent of full-blown flowers
Long days of sun - or gentle showers
July is the end of examination
Suitcases labelled for destinations
Far away for a week or so
Then home to water, weed and hoe
Traffic jams on a trip to the sea
Half a day there, then back for tea
'But please! One walk along the pier
The man with the sea urchins may be there'
'Well just one look, but hurry do
An early start and we'll miss the queue'
Bonfires burning on summer nights
The neighbours curse, the kids delight
The song of the bird, the buzz of the bee
These are the things July means to me.

A M Amos

DIVORCE

Divorce is sad for one and all,
For husband and wife, and especially the small,
After living together for many years,
A break-up can only mean lots of tears.

Children are unhappy when their parents part,
Not knowing what's happening could beak their hearts,
The worry is great for the working wife,
To know you will work for the rest of your life.
The children are resilient, and will get over it all,
But the long-term effect we will never know.

Solicitors, questions, green forms and white,
The Judge in the Court - a formidable sight.
What would we do without parents and friends?
Without their support we would go round the bend.
Unhappiness is permanent to only a few,
Good Luck to all, to start life anew.

Sue Finbow

So Perfect

Eyes so deep, so rare,
I feel myself drowning into a dreamy daze.

Eyes the colour of rich chocolate that melt into me,
as does butter in a frying pan.

Eyes that pull me in,
like metal to a magnet.

Eyes that glisten so bright,
as does the millions of stars
in the sky.

Eyes that remain in my mind,
as does the water in the ocean.

I close my eyes,
and that's where they'll be.

C Day

CONSEQUENCES

I watched the pain in her pale eyes,
Which slowly increased every day.
It was obvious she was dying,
For her mistake, she had to pay.

Painfully, she cried for help,
And reached out to me.
I could not bear thinking about,
How she was trapped and I was free -

She only wanted a 'normal' life
Not a million fears
I wanted my friend back
Not her tears . . .

She was now thin and frail,
Doctors said there was no hope.
Death was waiting for her,
And there was no way she could cope.

Her last word was 'Help,'
And then she slowly drifted away . . .
Even though she has died,
In my heart she will always stay.

Aids has slowly killed her,
And taken my friend away from me
But at least now I know
Her pain is gone, leaving her free.

Suraya Bashir

A Journey In Life

Silence has fallen
Upon my life
Feeling that I can no longer
Strife
My life has fallen upon a sadness
Drawing me deeper into darkness
I'm trying so hard to be strong
Hoping this journey will not
Be so long
The sun will shine at the end
Of this tunnel
Happiness flowing back through
My funnel
And though this will change
The feelings of sadness
Will it bring back my feeling
Of calmness.

Kathleen Reid

NOBODY TO TALK TO

Nobody understands me,
I find it so hard to explain.
I keep everything locked up inside,
And my worries still remain.
I've tried so many times,
To open-up to others.
I get so far, and then go quiet,
The rest is kept under covers.
No-one has ever took time-out,
To listen to what I've to say.
That's the way it's always been,
And probably the way it'll stay.
I need someone to talk to,
Someone to tell everything to.
But nobody's got time to listen,
They've all got things to do.

Leanne Frisby

HAPPINESS!

Some folks find it quite easily, and pounce on it with glee.
Whilst to some poor souls, it will always remain a mystery.
You may travel many highways, and search both near and wide.
Over country lanes, and cities, even on the ocean tide.
So once you find this precious thing, treat it with tender care.
Just in case it ever vanishes, when once you saw it resting there.
It takes on many disguises, you'll need all your wits at bay,
To make absolutely certain, if you hope it's here to stay!
Should you prove to be unlucky, and your life seems such a mess.
Indulge not in self-pity, there are other methods of success.
If you approach life with some courage, and a fair share
of unselfishness,
Then you'll find my friend, you've taken, the first steps to . . .
Happiness!

M Ross

CEASEFIRE

Please let there be a
Ceasefire in
Northern Ireland
For what does it
Gain
A part from only
Pain
To the families
Of victims who
Die
How can the
IRA
Just let them
Lie
After a
Bombing
Which people
Did not see
Coming

Coleen Bradshaw

NATURE'S BEAUTY

Nature's explosion brings
all that is new,
making each day a picturesque view,
They hung on horizons
still wet with the dew,
all things awaiting the God-given sun,
as up from the sea
it oft seems to come.
To warm and dry the painting that's done,
the beauty of nature
with its wonderful poise,
a wonderful gift of God's given joys.

V N King

EVERY SUCH THING

For every icy wind that blows
For every stranger that comes and goes
and every word a loved-one swears
For every brand-new life bared
For every breath that you take
For every mark that you make
and every tear a loved one sheds
For every brave soldier dead
For every star that shines
For every hopeful given sign
and every blooming flower
For every skyscraping tower
For every journey made
For every goodbye bade
and every child born
For every promise sworn
For every intentional harm
For every hand-reading palm
and every person's wish
For every special dish
For every guilty sinner
For each and every beginner
and every prior event
For every blessing sent
For every careless fault
For every clever thought
and every person's prayer
For every deed and dare
Just remember this as such
I love you a million times as much

Dear Friend

Mary Ibeh (15)

THE WISHING FISH

A long time ago I met a fish,
It said to me
'Make a wish'
So I wished for some money
And pots and pots full of honey
And then one day my fish said to me
'If you ever tell a lie
I'm afraid I'll have to die'
And that was it
I never lied
And so my fish stayed alive
And then one day I made a wish
I wished for something for my fish
I wished that he had another fish mate
And that I had a new shining, golden gate
But then one day I'm afraid I lied
And very tragically my fish, he died
Now I know not to lie
When I do I'm sure to cry.

Siân Jones

A MAN CALLED PHIL

I met a man one day,
He said to me
'Hi my name's Phil,
And I like watching The Bill.'
'Hi my name's Bryan,
Why are you crying?'
'I'm crying because
My uncle's dying.'
'Let's go to the wishing well.'
'Yes OK maybe my uncle Mel might get well.'
'It's a letter for me it says,
Dear Phil I've survived. Yes he's alive.'

Cheryl Jones (10)

SAVIOUR DEAR

Saviour dear to thee we pray
enfold us with your love alway.
Keep us safe where'er we be
your light to shine eternally.

Deep within our heart such peace
friendship so true never to cease.
Calmness soon will conquer fear
knowing that you are ever near.

Clouds of grey to fade and die
hopes to blossom reaching so high.
Healing hands to ease all pain
much courage shared then strength regain.

Faith too always by our side
patience, guidance, never denied.
Let your spirit gently fall
surround in glory one and all.

Margaret Jackson

THE GHOST OF WINTERS PAST

Where are the winters, the Christmas card winters?
Stars in the night sky, hard frost on the ground;
Children bright-eyed, the cold mitigated
By warm gloves and hats and anticipation
Of fun to be found at the party to come
At the house on the green silhouetted;
Where presents surround the tree in the corner
And lights in the window keep darkness at bay.

Pictures like this still arrive in December,
Traditional Christmases painted and drawn;
Large ones and small ones that bring 'Season's Greetings'
Stand on the window sills, hang from the walls -
As welcome a sight in our global-warmed home
As Giles's old grandma, boot-deep in snow.

Sheila Burnett

PARIS SUMMER 1997

After the Eiffel Tower the Louvre,
queues shuffling in the harsh sun;
then amid brief eddies the tow
of the stream sweeping past a blur
of damaged gods into the room
with one focus. A shadowed
woman watching from behind a glass pane.
And seething round, cameras and faces
being taken. Buffeting squalls
of smiles breaking and lost again.
And the picture seems commonplace
amid the pain and spirit on the walls.
Yet still behind the smile the siren calls.

David Ball

TOGETHER

When unveiled our hearts to those we love
May good fortune attend, perchance to love
Without default, allow your aching heart be healed
Endowed within your beauty, grace revealed.

For a heart, a soul, without deception plain
Through love's almighty vastness, life regain
Without intrigue corrupt, to you love brought,
Love of another without search, or sought.

For the voice of my heart would simple ask
Your hand in mine, your heart to clasp;
A hand which knows how to comfort much,
A hand so gentle, blessed its touch.

What other for me, but like an empty chalice bring,
A vessel not of love, with dried and empty ring;
But of warmth, joy, compassion, a holy sense to be
Would only right, the one be you for me.

J M H Barton

So Sad

It's so sad when someone dies
It's lonely for the wife
All she does is cry
Tears of heartache tears of pain
Never to see them again
No-one understands how you feel
Only you who hasn't a clue
How to start again you have to in the end.
Pick up the pieces bit by bit
Wondering why you and no-one else
Why did God take my *Dad*
He's the only one we ever had.
Mum misses him so it's hard to let go
We miss you so much your spirit will
Guide us through but what I'd give for
Another chance
To tell you *Dad* you were the *best*
I hope you deserved your well-earned rest
In my heart you'll stay
I know you were *brave* up until that very day

L Bevan

MY SHRINKING WORLD

My world has shrunk since Margaret died;
I go no more to Malvern.

Alice has left her Bewdley home;
no point in going there.
Jennett still lives in Keighley,
but the journey is too far.

There's no-one left in Warwick
of those I used to know'
There *are* still folk in Kenilworth,
but I'm not allowed to go.

So why don't I drive to Leamington,
accepting niece's plea?
Perhaps because here in Moseley,
is where I want to be:

contented, in my garden,
with books for company.

Geraldine Squires

ONLY FREEDOM CAN WHISPER

My bare, frozen feet tread over the coarse sand,
The fierce merciless breakers pound against the shore.
The rain beats down, like a hard, tensed-up hand,
And a lonely, solemn seagull calls out to me once more.

The cold, icy fingers of the wind, tangle through my hair.
Each raindrop stinging, like fire would burn.
The cliff hanging above me, looking proud, without care,
The menacing grin of the waves, loud, and stern.

The seaweed lies dead, and limp beside me,
As I slow to halt, looking at the textured floor.
My eyes drift over, to the tossed, troubled sea,
And a lonely, solemn seagull, calls out to me once more.

Kimberley Huggens (14)

FISH AND CHIPS

One of our favourite meals is -
fish and chips. Eating while -
sitting on the harbour wall.

Here we can sit and watch the -
boats go by. And decide which -
of them will be ours to sail -
the seas of the world.

The seagulls also have an interest -
in our fish and chips. And swoop -
to catch our leftovers.

In this interest each gull takes -
part in a race with the others.
To see who will catch the prize.

At the shop where we get our -
fish and chips, we get prize portions.
Yum, yum, yum.

Norman Mason

BOUQUET OF LILIES
(Dedicated to Mounir Murad)

Bouquet of lilies, an unfolded thought,
moistened with the sender's care, makes
our home a magic boat.

Does your short lifespan set here to rise there
in an unknown heaven filled with
secrets of scented prayer?

Your milky flames undulate and vibrate,
gradually doze and turn pallid
to make us meditate.

When shall you return to your family
perfectly stout and widely sheen
where you scent lyrically?

We always enjoy your cherished perfume,
but we don't notice the reason
why in our mind you bloom.

Bid us no farewell, life goes on in new
fashion; soon you'll sit back in white;
truth always stands anew.

Talk not to us about colour and scent
but your intuition and wisdom -
life's descent and ascent.

Keep perfuming our pen and paper world,
consoling broken hearts, making
poets voice your weird word.

We will try to reach out to your kingdom,
to dream of your celestial home;
let's beam in your wisdom.

You majestically play a symphony
of weird aroma; bless our soul
with peace and harmony.

Najwa Salam Brax

AGEING

Block up the frequencies
The long-wave transmitters
Blow out the cobwebs
Hose out the barn
Rock over the fields of clover
Remind the doves to coo again
Throw away the candyfloss
Unbutton the cigars
Push up the daisies
Put them in a vase

Blast out the shutters
Push away the cars
Break down the barricades
Empty out the coffee jars
Send out the semaphores
Eke out the wishing wells

Join up the dots
Shovel out the coal fire
Bring in the kryptonite
Ward off the banshee wail
Dim out the lights

Deliver us from evil
Return and take flight
Reach for the drawbridge
Dry out the moss
World always turning
Continents not lost.

Greg Smith

BIRDS DON'T FLY

I never knew a bird that flew,
instead they've walked right by
and though I cried they didn't have a clue.

I once observed them in a zoo
and there they didn't fly.
I never knew a bird that flew.

It's said they glide in skies of blue.
I guess they all have died,
and though I cried they didn't have a clue.

I always thought that I was due
to watch and see them soaring high.
I never knew a bird that flew.

They say it is a stunning view,
I really don't know why
and though I cried they didn't have a clue.

They say they fly and that it's true,
I though it was a lie.
I never knew a bird that flew
and though I cried they didn't have a clue.

Jonathan David Levine

UNSPOILT GRANDEUR

Glorious prospects spread round northern heights,
Farmsteads, bustling Tyne;
Durham Cathedral's famed timeless delights.
Farne Island's rare coastline,
Hadrian's Wall moorland for the trekker,
Vast Kielder Forest cheers the picnicker.

Breezy eastern counties with Norfolk Broads,
Spoonbill birds in summer;
Miles of waterways with sailing rewards,
Trips for each newcomer.
Finest windmills at Horsey and Reedham,
Single lane humped-back bridge Potter Heigham.

Southerly to Dorset's Chesil Bank's reef,
Golden arc of shingle;
Encloses lake with swannery motif,
Sixteen miles of pebbles intermingle.
Stormy seas pile gravel on a high bank,
Happy hunting, beachcombers on its flank.

Westward to Torbay's prime Riviera,
Lively harbour, blue sea.
Bright sailed yachts gliding for keen seafarer,
Packed attractions near quay.
Exotic palm house, sub-tropical trees,
Nine 'blue flag' beaches, boutiques for sightsees.

Land's End gale-swept Atlantic granite mass,
Longships Lighthouse on rock;
South West Coast Path, six hundred miles, alas
For those tied to the clock.
After gales, cliffs reflect superb rainbow;
In south-sheltered coves camellias grow.

James Leonard Clough

The Aardvark And The Snake

An aardvark looking for some food
Discovered ants to eat
Delicious hors d'ouvres were being served
So very small and sweet
'I say there ants, by any chance
I'd dearly love for us to meet'
The wise ants looked up high above
They knew not to dare
They rushed about their tiny house
Warning all in there
'There's an aardvark very close by
So darling ants take care'
A snake then crawled across the floor
And hissed to all close by
Both wide awake stood aardvark and snake
In the desert hot and dry
'Darling ants come out and dance
Underneath a pleasant sky'
The ants knew not to be so silly
As to fall for such a trick
They wrote a note and then let float
Tied to a balloon and stick
'We've decided to stay indoors today
I'm afraid we're all quite sick.'

Rodger Moir

RECIPE FOR MARRIAGE

Although love is the main ingredient
There are a few more besides this
If you want to live your life
In the happy state of married bliss
You cannot make this recipe without trust
Respect is an absolute must
Never substitute truth with lies
Add liberal amounts of compromise
An apology may be needed, in case you make a mistake
Keep a good stock of promises, they have a tendency to break
An argument won't spoil it, if understanding is added soon
Remember never to boil it, or it won't last beyond the honeymoon.

Heather Kirkpatrick

TRAVELLERS

Travelling together embodied in colour
Trails of fresh ground to cover
Scenery around draws out attention
Along the way so much beauty to mention

White horses slowly they're pulling along
Red and green caravans, the birds are in song
Hills, valleys, blue skies overhead
Fields of flowers for turning the head

Contentment was with them one and all
Leaf here and there downward did fall
Weary animals now ready to rest
To lie on green grass looking its best

Dog freely runs around and barks
Children together they're having a lark
Another day tomorrow, they will travel along
Contentment in hearts, the bond is strong.

Hannah Birch

TOGETHER FOREVER
(I dedicate my poem to my dear husband Franco)

We walked life's path, clasping hands together.
We met with stony ground.
We found the mystery of the land, in the journey that we'd planned.
We laughed, and rolled on the grass, with the gaiety of youth.
We kissed with such great passion, like the flame of the forest fire,
eager were our lips full of wild desire.
We met with many obstacles, and nearly lost our grip,
So we held on even tighter, still waiting were those lips.
The stream flowed with such magic, when the sun shone down,
picking up the ripples like gems from underground.
The journey is near to ending.
We walk on solid ground.
Should you meet us on our journey, you will always find,
our hands are clasped forever, wherever we are found.

M Rossi

RAINBOWS

Seven colours I could see across the world,
What could it be?
'Why a rainbow,'
Said an old man standing next to me.
Then we chatted merrily.
'God sent these pretty colours,
To remind us of what we see,
Each colour of the rainbow has a meaning,
Don't you see?
The red that looks so fierce is the blood within our veins.
The yellow that stands out brightly means winter, sun, and rain.
The pink tucked in beneath them, so bashful, timid and shy.
Is love that God has sent us, no further than our eye.
The green that lies so peaceful under dear God's watchful eye.
Means meadows, trees and grass and hills that reach up high.
The orange that stands out proudly is all our hearts desire,
To make our dreams and goals in life, grow rapid like a fire.
The purple that looks so dull and boring, are the mistakes
                                                    we make in life,
For I'm sure we have all made them, more than once or twice.
The last colour of the rainbow is pretty little blue,
That surrounds our heavenly angels, and mine and your world too.
All these colours put together,
Are to unite us in this world forever.'

Maria Babbington (14)

DEAR JOHN BIRT . . .
(A poet's plea to the DG of the BBC)

May I commend the 'super-editor',
Who decided to include,
The views of Tony Benn,
Which have *not* been understood?

Tony Blair's been 'out of order',
To *reject* Tony Benn,
And so to fail to include him,
In his social morals regimen.

Benn's statesmanship is not *perfect*,
But it is better far,
Than the wimpish USA adulation,
Of the *Lib Dem* legal star. (Ming Campbell)

These were the two main speakers,
In Channel One of Friday past
Which, I thought, quite *superior*,
To the usual BBC broadcast.

Benn was *justified* in *signalling*,
'Strikes' were an *'act of war'*,
By single 'sovereign nations',
Which USA and UK *leaders* think they are.

A 'multi-nation' planet
Is *a really massive wrong*
And *global integration,*
Must be our newest song,

There are *enemies* of global unity,
In the *new Labour government* today,
Like Robin Cook and Peter Shore,
Who *disapprove* what Benn will say.

But Benn's a better *Democrat*,
Than they will ever be,
For he's an anti-*lordship's* man,
And cares for *humanity*.

These verses are a *serious plea*,
To *you* to go on using *Benn*.
Give him a *spot* like *Kilroy*,
(And, to 'warring nations')
We will *one day say . . . Amen!*

Edward Graham Macfarlane

UNTITLED

She was lied to,
She was used,
She was beaten,
She was bruised,
She had nothing,
Not a thing,
She would do nothing but give,
You ask, for why did she live?
She never, ever hated,
She just waited,
For the love she deserved,
Only this was preserved,
For her to send,
As she came closer to an end.

Tracey Rush

LOST HALO

The beautiful moon.
Silver woman in the sky,
Someone's lost halo.

Marion Schoeberlein

HIDDEN SECRETS

In our world just now there is troubled times
as those terrorists commit their heinous crimes
They use explosives in their operations
causing countless deaths and devastation.

It is mostly innocents that they kill
the old and children who have no ill-will
They are cold and callous with their intentions
and as merciless killers are past redemption

They must have friends who know their names
to keep this hidden they must feel shame
To harbour killers that are strongly hated
their action can't ever be exonerated.

Lachlan Taylor

MY PRAYER FOR TODAY (FOR STRENGTH)

Arise and awaken Oh my soul and be glad
For the wonderful night's rest you have had.
Give thanks for the dawn of this new day
In which to love, to laugh, to work and to play.
As the sun rises high to shed its light
Make this my day to be kind and so right.
Let the love of God that is in my heart,
Pour forth on all of whom I am a part.
So . . . when the sun sets in the golden west
I can thank God today, I did my very best.

William Price

AND ALL I ASK

Pebbles dancing on the beach,
Tossed ashore by an angry wave.
And still somehow you're out of reach.
And am I forgotten, in this unmarked grave.

Why can't you see me from the shore?
I am always here, be it night or day.
And all I ask and nothing more,
Is to be with my loved ones every day.

I'm a long-lost soul who drowned at sea,
And still my spirit flows aimlessly,
And all I ask and nothing more,
Is to be with my loved ones whom I adore.

In nineteen twelve on that fateful night,
I was aboard a ship, which disappeared from sight,
And all I ask and nothing more,
Is to be with my loved ones, forever more.

Eddie Jepson

ONE WOMAN'S PAINS! ONE WOMAN'S JOY!

In my waking life
every destination
A fear of loneliness
each shiver of loneliness
A deep pain
every hurtful pain
A sacred tear
gone not forgotten
An escape far away
in a make believe paradise
of imagination going crazy
A step to far out of reality
paradise where tears
precious as wine
Paradise of desires
each desire achieved
Paradise every dove with
A message of love for me
My paradise of love
each love unique and treasured
A paradise where each
pain as hurtful as a
Delicate rose falling from
the velvet sky
Paradise each star in the
dark sky, a diamond for me.

Saiqah Salim

My Friend Knows

They say my friend has a big nose.
He takes it with him wherever he goes.
It's six feet long and one foot thick.
He wields it like a mighty stick.

But this of course is a load of bunk,
The proper word is 'elephant's trunk'.
With sixty thousand muscles, it really has to work,
There's not so many chores that an elephant can shirk.
Build bridges, stack timber and even uproot trees.
But be sure that you stand clear, if he has to sneeze.

The tip is sensitive, to discover shape and texture.
He can pick up, and uncork a bottle, even taste the mixture
He can curl it around a pencil, to write his friend a note.
He can use it to remove a thorn, sticking in his throat.

He can hold an egg quite tight, and not even break it.
But only another elephant would dare to try to take it.
He can powder his body with dust.
Or take a shower anytime that he must.
Walk on a river bed, with a gay chortle,
Using his enormous trunk as a snorkel.

He can talk to his friends by: trumpeting,
Humming, roaring, piping, purring,
Rumbling and noisily rattling
His trunk against the ground.

He can smell a python hidden in the grass.
Quickly step aside, so to let it pass.
And smell food a mile away . . . any time, any day.
He can do most anything. But only my friend knows:
There's just one thing that he *can't* do:
My friend can't pick his nose.

Stu Phillips

WAITING

Waiting, waiting, waiting
Waiting for a brand-new life
My hope's evaporating
Waiting for the surgeons' knife

It isn't fair, do they really care?
Is it right I should live in pain?
If I could pay somehow they would heal me now
And I could lose my ball and chain.

Called in to talk but it's hard to walk
On legs with arthritic ache
First they set a date but then I'm told to wait
Here's another pill to take.

Will they operate or is it my fate
To go on in this living Hell
If I can't stem the pain I think I'll go insane
And there's no-one left to tell.

Waiting, waiting, waiting
Waiting for that healing touch
My life just goes on wasting
I'll pay, just find out how much!

M Shimmin

FOOTPRINTS

Now she sits beside the window
Just passing her days.
Alone with those memories
of better days.
Now she never goes down
to the beach any more
So her wet footprints are no longer
to be found near to the shore
There was a time when she used to
wait for the sea to call out her name
once more
And the lonely cry of the seagulls
As they fly above in the sky
shaped her fate.
For she could never wait
to be beside her lover the sea
once more.
Just to leave her wet footprints
close to the shore
For others who may wish to follow.

K Lake

THE WIDOWER CRIES

How can the years have gone
Since first we met and wed?
How can it seem so hopelessly long
Since we nightly shared our bed?
Where is the love each had for each,
And the treasure of meeting minds?
How has it all gone out of reach
Like the daylight when darkness blinds?
How I long for the sun of your life to shine,
Warming the life that's gone cold!
Joining your lips and your arms to mine
When it seemed we could never grow old.
I feel that I want to follow you, dear,
Yet I know it's a cowardly way.
So I must just swallow my fear
And live on from day to day.
But it's going to be terribly hard to do
When there's none to cheer me on,
And all my days left I will grieve for you
Till myself and my grief are gone.

Rannoch Melville Russell

MAKE THE MOST OF EACH NEW DAY

Make the most
of each new
day.

Then you will
receive your
pay

Happiness
will follow you

Like a skylark
in the blue.

David Bray

MEMORIES

Memories harness values
Reason for remembrance
Awake or entwined in precious dreams
Partnership with love and friendship
Hurtful, joyous, peacefulness
All play a vital part of growth
Memories freely filter through
Stabilising many a mood, to remain true.

Alan Jones

LIKE A SAD SONG

I listened to a sad song, my laughter turned to tears,
No lightness in my spirit but many lonely fears
I tried to think of good things but all I felt was pain
So many troubled people and all they knew was rain.

They bore the scars and bruises of hurts within their lives
Their minds were blocked and shattered, their hearts were filled
with knives,
I thought of Enniskillen; Omagh and of Lockerbie
I knew there was an answer; I knew who held the key.

I listened to a sad song of Jesus on the cross
The saddest durge of all time, the greatest ever loss
My heart revived within me; my soul took on fresh hope,
These people needed Jesus - not left alone to cope.

I realised time is running out; the days are getting short,
No hope for all the Nations unless Good News is brought
And we must sing our Love Song or it'll be too late,
Not leave them to the devil and leave them to their fate.

God will give them laughter, a New Song within their hearts
Their sins will be forgiven and blotted from the past,
New life will dawn upon them - the Holy Spirit's power
A bud at first shall open then blossom like a flower.

I saw my life in stages as though groping for a light,
I'd searched. I'd strived. I'd struggled. It had been a fight,
I'd looked in many places. I'd travelled many paths.
The *only* way was Jesus. Only He can change our hearts.

I thought of life without Him - I guess at death we'd die!
He gave His life for many. 'It is finished' was that cry
A cry that had no answer from His Father up above
But God looked down upon His Son and all He saw was love.

I listened to that Love Song and yet I still felt sad
A chord played deep within me; this world has just gone mad
We've got this power to tell them, yet there's a price to pay
Are we prepared to pay that price or go on our sweet way?

Judy Studd

THE PICTURES

This is a good one on
The wall - an oil of ships
At sea; look at the sun
On the water - Dad brought
That back from Gibraltar.

Here is a photo of Uncle
Joe - a mezzotint, then it
Was all the go. You don't
See that kind of thing
Now. This one's interesting
It shows a cow. That
Was first prize at the
County fair.

This one's my mum and
Dad and your Aunty Clair.
Grandad in Ireland, Susan
On the beach and there -
A lovely little water-colour
Of wild flowers. You children
Used to play for hours: in
The garden where I planted
Them.

David Hazlett